MOVE

You're In the Way of Your Own Destiny

Tishawa Howard

www.tishawahoward.com

Copyright © 2019 by Tishawa Howard

All rights reserved. No part of this publication may be reproduced, stored in retrieval system, or transmitted in any form or by any means electronic, mechanical, photocopying, recording, or otherwise without prior written permission of the publisher.

Published by:
Tishawa Howard, LLC
PO Box 551820
Miami Gardens, FL 33055

MOVE – You're in the Way of Your Own Destiny

ISBN: 978-1-7344040-0-5

For Worldwide Distribution, Printed in the U.S.A.

Front and Back Cover Design by Dee McIntosh
Front and Back Photo Credit: Mark Hill Photography

www.tishawahoward.com

Tributes

My mother is a selfless, caring, passionate, loving, incredible person. Someone who worries about taking care of others before herself. Someone that gets excited at the mere fact that she has made the next person smile. She doesn't ask for much, but always wants the best for people. She holds herself to such a high standard and does not break that character for anyone. All in all, she is someone to be admired and revered for her work ethic and relentless will to win.

Donte' Howard, *Son*

Tishawa is a mother, sister, daughter, successful businesswoman, a child of God and many more titles to her name. She is someone who I admire and appreciate.

As a young single mother, she did not allow fear to stop her dreams. She trusted God and stepped out on faith by leaving a secure stable job to start her own business. She did not know the plans that God had for her life, but she trusted Him and He has provided and established connections for her along her journey.

Tishawa is an inspiration to her family and friends and provides encouragement to everyone she meets to reach their full potential.

I am so proud of the woman she has become. I love you.

Sophia Henry, *Sister*

With a long track record of excellence and an enormous capacity to raise the standard, Tishawa Howard has been a beacon of strength, stability and courage to her community, co-laborers and to all whom she encounters. Never shrinking down to challenges, her tenacity to excel to the next level inspires onlookers to reach higher to achieve purpose and destiny.

Through informative and inspirational seminars, conferences, life-changing coaching and masterful financial strategies, Tishawa is leading the way in helping countless people live their best life now.

We've heard the saying that we are our own worst enemy. This book not only reveals the truth behind those words but equips us with proven strategies to transform us from being an enemy to ourselves to being our greatest ally. Deciding to be successful requires courage. By sharing her personal journey, Tishawa gives insight into the process of moving forward and brings to life the principles that govern maximized living.

Pastor Austin Darling, Jr.
Senior Pastor,
Jesus People Victorious Living Church

I met the author Tishawa Howard over 25 years ago, while on her search for truth, wisdom and knowledge of God's purpose for her life. I was graced with the privilege to be called by her, "spiritual mother." Her loyalty, commitment and service in the Kingdom of God is the platform from which this great work, "Move... You're in the Way of Your Own Destiny" was birthed. Her diligence, determination, and resilience will be revealed in each chapter.

Tishawa has always had a heart and desire to see others live their best life. She made the decision to leave a very lucrative and comfortable job to become an entrepreneur almost 20 years ago because as she stated, "I want to help people and especially the body of Christ build wealth and an inheritance for their generations." I have watched her successfully enrich, instruct, and empower others to build financial security through conferences, group trainings, and individual sessions.

Tishawa, through this book, will challenge you to keep moving by doing the work necessary to complete your assignment. She will motivate you through this writing to never give up and stay focused in the middle of the struggle until you begin to thrive. I am sure when you've finished this book you will be able to apply these very practical principles to start, continue, or finish what's in your heart (business, book, ministry) for your generations.

Congratulations Tishawa for trusting the process, being transparent, and overcoming every distraction to this very important work. I pray God's manifold blessings on this work and the readers for generations to come. Families will prosper and be in good health even as their souls prosper (3 John 1:2).

"Get ready. Take a seat. Look at what courage sounds like. See how valiant it is to reveal yourself in this way. But above all, see what it is to thrive, to deeply influence the lives of others after walking out your truth."

Minister Barbara A. Hunter
Spiritual Mother

Foreword

It is an extraordinary thing to find a person who is willing to pull back the curtain of their private life and invite the world to get a glimpse of what so many strive to conceal. Global platforms, through various media streams, often compel us to project only the "good stuff."

However, when I read the manuscript for this book *Move, You're in the Way of Your Own Destiny* by Tishawa Howard, I felt a sense of refreshing. I was also made to realize that every day is a new day in which I could decide to get out of my own way and win.

I have known Author, Tishawa Howard for many years, which has given me the unique opportunity to see her transition from one level to the next. She is indeed a genius abounding with wisdom beyond her years. I am proud to have been asked to write the foreword for this literary work. I know the realness of Tishawa's story and applaud her for reaching back to help others overcome their challenges.

As an Author, Columnist and Blogger, I am always excited to read literature that shifts my paradigm and this book does that. Readers will be motivated to expand their mindset and take a fearless leap of faith into the unknown. *Move, You're in the Way of Your Own Destiny* by Tishawa Howard is the perfect tool for awakening the reader's hunger and thirst for more.

I spend much time building my knowledge base about many areas of life and I am proud to have access to the principles in this book. This work encourages the reader to think beyond the narrative of their past experiences and imagine how wonderful life could be if they wrote the ending to their own story.

Move, You're in the Way of Your Own Destiny by Tishawa Howard is loaded with real-life experiences as well as practical tips to assist the reader as they get out of their own way. The prominent theme entrenched in this work is that, regardless of external roadblocks and push back, each individual has within them the power to change their own world.

Tishawa Howard can be assured that there will be countless grateful readers who will get inspired to go further than they ever have, by equipping themselves with the priceless concepts presented in *Move, You're in the Way of Your Own Destiny*.

Natalie B. Green
Author, Speaker, Coach, Mentor
Deeper Still with Natalie Green
Miami Gardens, FL

Table of Content

Introduction 1

Chapter 1: Being Comfortable 3

Chapter 2: The Transformation 9

Chapter 3: Enjoy the Journey 15

Chapter 4: Don't let the Stress Kill You 21

Chapter 5: Be Committed to You 25

Chapter 6: Believe in You 29

Chapter 7: Doing it Again 33

Chapter 8: Passing the Torch 39

About the Author 43

Dedication 45

Contact Information 49

Introduction

I believe that everyone has a gift that is to be used to impact their household, community, nation or the world. My question has always been why do some people maximize their gifts to the fullest, others half way, and still others not at all?

As I pondered this question and reflected on my own journey from corporate America to being an entrepreneur, I realized that anything I gained or didn't obtain was because of ME. There is nothing that can hold me back but ME. That doesn't mean that there aren't any challenges, obstacles or roadblocks, but it does mean that I can't allow those things to stop me from being my best me.

I have met hundreds of people from different fields that have embarked on the road to entrepreneurship as well; and there has been commonality such as working hard, discipline, knowing your craft, and consistency. However, some still experienced failures in their businesses, ministries or other leadership roles which have its own commonalities such as lack of self-confidence, overburden with fear, or unbelief in oneself.

It is with this latter statement that this book is birthed. I realized that those that became successful had similar fears and failures but they pushed through the fears to win anyway. I further realized that the biggest battle came through personal thoughts when alone. Thus, I chose to be transparent to empower the reader to confront oneself in their thinking and move forward.

To get the fullness of the book, take the time after each chapter to meditate, do a self-examination, be honest with yourself and decide to change what needs to change. And if you're really serious about the change, obtain and assign accountability partners.

Each chapter stands alone, so it can be kept in your "**go-to**" arsenal as a quick reminder in the area needing a boost.

We can't conquer what we don't confront and there are plenty of television shows, podcasts, and events that are about Real Talks. And the best Real Talk you or I can have is the one that we have with ourselves. Let's commit to continuously having those talks and then do what it takes to present our gifts to the World. If not you, then who?

Think of it this way, we only have one life to live, so let's get out of our own way and live it!

Tishawa

Chapter 1

BEING COMFORTABLE

I had been working for the Internal Revenue Service for almost 10 years when I was placed in charge of the Volunteer Income Tax Assistance Program (VITA) for the north part of Miami-Dade County. I fell in love with the program and the volunteers so much that I worked nights and weekends to ensure its success. It was a great feeling of accomplishment because in this position I was helping taxpayers and they were grateful for the help. This was different from my normal duties as a Revenue Agent which was auditing businesses and letting them know that they owed more in taxes.

At the end of the year, annual evaluations were due. As is customary, I prepared my evaluation and my immediate supervisor agreed that the work I was doing deserved increases in the evaluation. He sent the paperwork to his superior, which was required for final approval. A few weeks later I was excited to go to his office to discuss the results, only to be told that the evaluation would not be signed, as it would put me next in line for a promotion.

As I was stuck in a slow-motion daze of what I was hearing, I began to feel baffled, hurt, confused, angry and an exponential state of disbelief all at the same time. My world was spinning as I was trying to comprehend the words that were being spoken. At the same time, I was thinking, *"how did I get here?"* How did I get to a place where an increase in an evaluation controlled my promotion, which controlled my paycheck, which controlled where I lived, the car I would drive and how I would provide for my son as a single mom.

As I continued to stand there, my thoughts then took me back to my interview while in college for the job:

> I only went to the interview to sharpen my interviewing skills. At the end of the interview, I was offered the job. With boldness, I stated that I was not interested in the job because I couldn't believe that people actually went to school to get an Accounting Degree to work for the IRS. With an utter surprise at my response, I was then asked, *"Well, what do you want to do?"* I stated I was getting my Bachelor's Degree, will obtain my CPA License, and then would own my own Accounting firm. They then stated that if I came and worked for them that I would get free education on tax law for 5 years and when I left the IRS I could use my experience as a marketing advantage over other Accounting firms. With excitement, I said … "Ok!!!"

As the years came and went, I loved the fact that I worked 7:00am - 3:30pm, had every weekend off, 6 weeks of vacation pay and 4 weeks of sick leave. The benefits were great, plus, I only had to come to the office once every 2 weeks and I worked at home most Fridays!

As the slow motion of my manager's conversation came to an end, I realized that I got into this position because I became comfortable. I forsook the goals and dreams to become an entrepreneur as a teenager for the comfort of a good job with benefits. It was in that moment I saw the thumb that I allowed to be placed on my neck and I said to myself I never want to be in this position again. Maya Angelou said, *"If you don't like something change it."* I decided that I would no longer look for a way up but for a way out!

Getting Out of Your Own Way:

List ALL the things that you are comfortable with but you know that you shouldn't be.

_____

_____

_____

_____

_____

_____

_____

Of those things, which are the Top 3 you need to change the most?

_____

_____

_____

_____

If you decide to become uncomfortable and make the necessary changes, give full details of what your life would look like?

_____

_____

_____

_____

_____

_____

_____

_____

_____

_____

_____

Chapter 2

THE TRANSFORMATION

But what should I do? I no longer desired to own my own CPA firm as I found Accounting to be very boring. Well, 3 weeks later I was introduced to Finances, the Rule of 72 and how to make my money grow. I was intrigued and embarrassed that I had an Accounting Degree and audited businesses but I had no education on how to get my money to grow for me. I was fully invested in my Thrift Savings Plan but my investment choices were solely based on what the senior agents were doing for themselves.

If I don't know how to get my money to grow and I think I'm smart, how many other people don't know how to get their money to grow? I chose to get out of my comfort zone, embark on something new and get back on track to becoming an entrepreneur.

I knew nothing of finances. All of my education and training had been in accounting. I did not let that stop me from embarking on this new path.

I committed myself to learning not just to get the required licenses but going home every night and putting the VHS tapes in the VCR and started to learn about the financial industry before I fell asleep.

When I was in my car, I would listen to tapes of people who had succeeded in this industry over and over again. I was hungry for the knowledge and I wanted to provide good service to my clients. So I worked on myself.

I changed my appearance. I didn't like business attire. I preferred to be comfortable with jeans and a nice top. At the IRS my badge authority required taxpayers to listen to me but not so as an Advisor. I started paying to get my nails done and I got a cell phone which was not common for everyone to have at that time. I understood that when you're in the sales industry first impressions are everything and you don't get a second chance to make a good first impression.

When I got my licenses, I made a decision to track the first 25 appointments. I did not beat myself up when someone told me NO; neither did I cheer too loud when someone told me YES. I chose to internalize each of those appointments as a learning lesson to do better for the next appointment. Through that exercise, I realized that I learned more when someone told me NO than when they said YES because it forced me to truly evaluate the appointment and work on bettering myself.

I was totally focused on building my confidence so that I could succeed in this new industry. I scheduled appointments whenever I could get them and took time off from work to go on them. I no longer saved my annual leave time to take off a month at a time but utilized the annual leave time I had to build my business. I found myself disconnecting from the thought process of being a star agent and instead focused on being a star for myself.

Almost a year later, I put in my resignation letter. Although I was excited about embarking on this new chapter, I was beginning to feel the doubt and fear of wondering if I could make it on my own. In spite of it, I took steps every day to get closer to my dreams. As if they could sense the fear, management asked me to just put in a one year leave of absence so that I would have something to fall back on. I thought about it for a quick second and said, "No, this is it! I'm going to put my faith in me and if I fail, I fail but I won't be back here or work for anyone else."

That was almost 20 years ago and now having been my own Boss for 19 of those years, I'm ecstatic that I chose to become uncomfortable and started the transformation.

Getting Out of Your Own Way:

What steps do you need to take to start your transformation?

_____

_____

_____

_____

_____

_____

_____

_____

Are you going to take those steps?

_____

If yes, When?

_____

Who will be your accountability partners to help you stay focused on those steps when you want to run back to being comfortable instead of completing your transformation?

_____

_____

_____

_____

_____

_____

_____

_____

Chapter 3

ENJOY THE JOURNEY

When you're a go-getter or someone that makes things happen, you tend to focus on the destination; the end goal. But when you do that, it is easy to miss the simple blessings, lessons, and pleasures of life.

It was an early Wednesday afternoon and I was having lunch with a millionaire and his wife at a resort on the water in Boca Raton, FL. While having lunch, I was complaining about my business. He stopped me and asked me the following:

- *"Tishawa, where are you?"* With my eyes looking around thinking it's a trick question, I responded, *"I'm here at the resort having lunch with the two of you."*
- *"What day of the week is it?"* Still not understanding these questions stated, *"Wednesday."*
- *"Who did you call to get permission when I asked you to come up her today?"* With eyes wide open, I said, *"uhhh... No one."*

- *"Who will you have to call when you stay longer than you thought?" "No one."*
- *"How much money did you make last month?" "Over $10,000."*

His response, "What's wrong with you Woman!!! Don't you realize that you are in the top 10% of the population! It's Wednesday, you control your time, you answer to no one and you're making money. Do you know what your problem is? You don't know how to enjoy the journey!"

With tears rolling down my face, I realized that I didn't.

I left that day determined to change. I found out my sister had a girls trip with her friends planned to Jamaica and I inserted myself on the trip. I almost chose not to go when I found out the dates were at the end of the month because when you're in sales, the end of the month is the worst time to be away. How can I be out of town at such a crucial time?! I worked hard, my team worked hard; and when I left I said if what I've built can't finish the job without me, I have a lot more building to do when I get back. I was nervous having never done this before but when I got to Jamaica I refused to purchase any type of phone or service that would allow me to keep in touch. I reached out one time (I couldn't resist) through my sister's phone and one of my leaders said, *"We got this… ENJOY your vacation!"* And that's what I did and for the 1st time in years, I totally unplugged mentally and breathed. Although I had been on plenty of trips, I finally allowed myself to be fully present on my vacation. I had a blast and when I returned, I learned that **Our Team Hit Our Goals!!!**

Getting Out of Your Own Way:

Taking time to unplug and relax is very important for self-care. How often do you do that?

_____

_____

_____

_____

_____

If you haven't been doing it, how often will you begin to do it?

_____

_____

_____

_____

List some of the things you will do while ensuring that you are fully enjoying the moment.

_____

_____

_____

_____

_____

_____

When are you going to start each activity?

_____

_____

_____

_____

_____

Chapter 4

DON'T LET THE STRESS KILL YOU

For about 60-90 days I was constantly tired. When I went to my primary physician all the reports were fine but the lethargy continued. My energy was drained. I woke up tired. I did whatever I had to do for the day and then went home as soon as I could.

Because I could feel myself deteriorating and the doctors couldn't find anything wrong, I decided to go to a holistic doctor. I took several tests. When he came back with the results, he looked at me with fear/disbelief in his eyes that I was still alive. My charts were 90% red! He said, *"you are overly stressed."* He further went on to say, *"because you are a business owner it comes with a certain level of stress which is not totally bad, but you are overly stressed."*

He said, *"I'm not sure what's all going on with you so we have to get to the root, but in the meantime, you can only watch movies that will make you laugh; no drama or emotional movies that would make you cry and you can only wear flower-based perfumes so that it uplifts you."* These were simple instructions but life-changing.

As I began to deal with the root I realized that I stressed over things that I couldn't control.

I had to learn to let things go. I had to learn to breathe. I had to learn to relax. I had to learn to smell the roses. I had to learn to appreciate what I do have. I had to learn to stop over-thinking things. I had to learn to walk away. I had to learn that I can't change people.

I must admit that I don't always remember to do what I learned which is why I periodically evaluate the temperature in my life and let go of things that have crept in to create stress. I remind myself that I almost died from this silent killer and thus there is no need for me to die early because I'm stressed out over people, opinions or things.

Getting Out of Your Own Way:

List people or situations that are totally stressing you out:

_____

_____

_____

_____

_____

_____

_____

What is in you that has allowed these people or situations to become a stress to you?

_____

_____

_____

_____

_____

You can't change people but you can change you. What things can you do to reduce or eliminate these stresses?

_____

_____

_____

_____

_____

_____

_____

Who will be your accountability partners to help you check your stress meter?

_____

_____

_____

Chapter 5

BE COMMITTED TO YOU

One day I was extremely exhausted from working but I got dressed to show up for an event that I had committed to. While driving on the way there, I had an epiphany: I was going somewhere I didn't feel like going anymore because I was tired but more importantly because I had given my word.

The epiphany was that when I commit to someone whether it's a friendship, relationship, coach or teammate I go the extra mile by doing whatever it takes to fulfill that commitment. But why when it's a commitment to myself, I don't work as hard?

As I pondered that fact, I was reminded that we are to love God with all of our hearts, soul and mind and then to love others as ourselves. The key is as **OURSELVES**. We are supposed to be committed to the dreams, visions, and goals that God has given us for our lives more than we are committed to someone else's. This sounds so selfish and can easily lead to an internal conflict. However, how can I truly be effective in another person's life if I don't walk in the fullness of mine? Let's look at it like this: How can I take care of your yard when I haven't taken care of my own? If I was a landscaper and you passed by my house and the grass was brown, overgrown and weeds were everywhere; would you have second thoughts about hiring me to be your landscaper? What if I was a personal trainer and I was 4x overweight for my height, no muscles or physique? Would you hire me to be your personal trainer? NO! So how can I be more committed to you than I am to myself? How can I tell you that you have what it takes to WIN and behind closed doors I tell myself I'm not worthy of winning.

Likewise, I had to make a decision to stop letting the world and false humility keep me from being my **Best Me**. I can only be my Best Me when I'm committed to being my Best Me for Me.

Once you have made the decision to be committed to you, it's time to do the work. It's time to research what's required to be successful. It's time to get the knowledge, education and skills. It's time to be a student. It's time to glean from those who have gone before you through books, CD's or mentorship. It's time to work while you're learning. **It's Time to MOVE!**

Getting Out of Your Own Way:

Being involved in different activities bring fulfillment. List ALL the things that you are committed to right now:

_____

_____

_____

_____

_____

Prioritize the list:

_____

_____

_____

_____

_____

List the Top 3 that fully aligns with your destiny:

_____

_____

_____

Identify the ones that you know you need to un-commit to or delegate to someone else:

_____

_____

_____

_____

_____

Chapter 6

BELIEVE IN YOU

Anytime you decide to go to another level, you have to go deeper inside of you to pull out more belief in yourself.

I remember feeling stuck, so I hired a business mentor. She stated that I had no presence in the marketplace so I had to create it. In less than 60 days, I had a logo, website, professional pictures and weekly tips on social media. I was amazed by all the positive feedback and that people really thought I was just now starting a new business!

By the third month, my mentor stated, *"Tishawa, you need to do a Conference."* I immediately rejected the thought and said, **"the devil is a liar…. we're not here for that. We are here for this, this and that!"** Within the next 2 weeks, I started having visions on having a Conference of what it would entail. I could not rest and I said, **"Lord, if it is You, I'll do it. I don't want to stop what You're doing in my life."** As I continued to meditate, I asked myself why did I immediately dismiss the thought and I realized that fear had gripped me. I had subconsciously said to myself *"I'm not Sara Jakes or Oprah Winfrey. Who am I that I could have a Conference and that people would come?"* So, it was easier to reject the whole idea than to have people reject me.

As I prepared to meet with my mentor again, I said, "Guess what? We're having a Conference!" She was soooo ecstatic. We immediately started planning. We looked at the calendar for dates, researched what the name would be, sought out a logical venue, determined the ticket prices, etc. From the time I said YES, the Conference was planned in 6 weeks. Everything and all the Speakers I wanted said YES! I was in TOTAL shock at how something I initially rejected not only was planned easily, but when the Conference was held we had sold almost 100 tickets. Those in attendance were awestruck at the spirit of excellence and said it was underpriced for the value. The speakers received A1 service, all of the vendors made money and business owners were highlighted. Many continuously gave testimonies on how the Conference pushed them to start a business, build additional streams of income, take classes and simply get out of the box and out of their own way.

With all the success that unfolded, what if I had continued to say NO due to my lack of belief in myself?

Getting Out of Your Own Way:

What thoughts and ideas have been presented to you that you rejected because of your lack of belief?

_____

_____

_____

_____

_____

_____

Are you going to work on your belief and *Go For It?*

_____

If yes, when?

_____

What steps are you going to take to get it done and who will hold you accountable?

_____

_____

_____

_____

_____

_____

_____

_____

Chapter 7

DOING IT AGAIN

Sometimes when you're building a business and you're going and going and grinding in the trenches, you can get burned out.

Burnout is when you want to but can't. The drive is gone. The passion, work ethic and consistency fades even though you're doing what you're called to do.

When I found myself in this season, I didn't go willingly but most of the reasons for doing the business were already accomplished and I no longer had a clear vision that drove me as to why I was doing it now. It was in this season I did a lot of self-reflection and evaluation.

I began to deal with issues I had ignored internally and that I thought would go away. I started working on my Total Wholeness. It was during this time that I began to confront **"ME."** I recognized the different weights I was carrying, the anger and brokenness that I held within because of past events. I got a counselor who helped me to not only recognize the traumas that were affecting my decisions, but gave me tools on how to deal with them so that it wouldn't cripple my future. I realized that because of the pressures to be a good leader in the home, church and business arenas, it is important to make mental wholeness a priority.

As I began to walk in my mental/emotional healing, I was told, *"You have been at this mountain tooo long… it's time to **Move!**"* As I began to move, it became evident to me that I no longer believed in myself to the high level that I once did. A real internal conflict evolved: on the outside, I was puffing my chest out because of all my past accomplishments but on the inside, I didn't believe I could not only do it again but exponentially surpass it.

So I started investing more time listening to recordings that would work on my mindset, attending trainings, getting multiple mentors that would breathe belief into me and challenge me to take the next step, and then the next, and then the next.

Now, I am at a point in which although I haven't fully arrived at my destination, all the weights have been lifted, a clear vision has returned. I am filled with Excitement to see ALL that I will Conquer just because I believe I can and I am no longer in my Own Way.

Getting Out of Your Own Way:

What is holding you back?

_____

_____

_____

_____

_____

_____

_____

_____

_____

_____

_____

What do you need to do to push past the fear and do it anyway?

_____

_____

_____

_____

_____

_____

Time is the only thing we cannot get back. When will you start moving forward?

_____

_____

_____

_____

_____

_____

Who you have in your circle is everything. List all the accountability partners, cheerleaders, and mentors that you will enlist on your journey to being your **Best You**:

_____

_____

_____

_____

_____

_____

_____

_____

_____

_____

Chapter 8

PASSING THE TORCH

Having helped hundreds of business owners and being a business owner myself, I realize that we can get so focused on the grind of building the business that it can be easy to forget to prepare for wealth sustainability and transference. Thus, as you are growing your business, you should ask yourself some of the following questions:

> *What is my exit strategy?*
> *What is the projected future value of my business?*
> *What if I get sick for an extended period of time?*
> *Will I have enough assets to retire comfortably?*
> *Who will be my successor/s?*

As you answer these questions, here is a comprehensive but not all-inclusive checklist to accomplish that:

- Emergency Fund Accounts
- Retirement Accounts
- Legal Will
- Trust (to avoid Probate Court)

- Living Trust
- Health Care Directives
- Durable Power of Attorney for Health and Finances
- Life Insurance Policies for Business and Personal
- Disability Policies
- Beneficiaries listed and annually updated on ALL Checking, Savings and Investment Accounts
- Safe Deposit Box Information
- List of ALL assets in a Secure Place

It is important to properly prepare for succession in business, ministry and personal so that each entity can continue to endlessly thrive.

Also, I have learned that some things are bought, sought, taught and caught.

As you prepare for a successful succession, teach your loved ones, business partners, and mentees how to do what you do while being their best selves. Allow them to spend time with you and have countless of conversations so that they can catch your spirit and thus, the greatest asset, which is **YOU** continues to live for generations to come.

Getting Out of Your Own Way:

Paint an extensive picture of how you want your business to operate when you retire or expire?

_____

_____

_____

_____

_____

What steps do you need to put in place to ensure the Vision you just painted happens?

_____

_____

_____

_____

_____

_____

Identify the people you want to mentor and pour in to and list beside each person how you want to influence their lives:

_____

_____

_____

_____

_____

_____

Evaluate your legacy plan in every area of your life and list what you need to do to implement it immediately:

_____

_____

_____

_____

_____

About the Author

Tishawa got a taste of entrepreneurship while in middle school, where she sold Blow Pops to her classmates. Her appetite for it was increased during High School, when she worked for an Accounting firm and noticed the freedom that her boss had. It was this desire that motivated her to get her Bachelors in Science Degree in Accounting at West Virginia State University. While at WVSU, she was not only hired with the government as an intern, but she also became a member of Delta Sigma Theta Sorority, Inc. through the Alpha Delta Chapter.

After working for the government for nearly 10 years, she finally reconnected with her passion of entrepreneurship, which she pursued by obtaining her professional licenses as a financial advisor and a certified business coach. Among her many accolades, she sits on the board of Family Christian Association of America, Inc., and was listed as one of the Top 25 Most Influential and Prominent Black Women in Business and Industry in South Florida.

Over the years, she has empowered people to take control of their finances and create a legacy through seminars for various businesses, non-profit organizations, churches, families and individual sessions.

Tishawa was born in Brooklyn, New York and is a first-generation American, born to Jamaican parents. She was raised in Miami, FL where she still resides. She enjoys spending time with her family, in which she is the eldest of her siblings, and has one son, Donte'.

DEDICATION

Move…You're in the Way of Your Own Destiny is dedicated to several people who have impacted my life by challenging and encouraging me to do my best.

To my father, **Lancelot Campbell:** Daddy, you have always been very intelligent and I always knew that if I had a technical question you would be able to help me solve it. I remember getting a "C" in one of my classes in High School and it was totally unacceptable to you. I was very upset that you would get so mad, but it instilled in me the desire to fight to do my best in everything. Thank you for being my sidekick in business and being selfless in helping it to grow.

To my mother, **Claudia Dacres:** God truly blessed my life when He chose you to be my mommy. You are the warmest, most giving, unselfish person that I know. Oh how I used to get mad when it seemed like you always took in strangers but it taught me not to look down on others because situations are temporary. It taught me that even when you don't have much, you can still find something to share. You have always poured belief in to me and told me that I can be whatever I wanted to be and that no one could stop me but me. Thank you for your love, hugs, kisses and the safety of your arms.

To my dad, **Peter Dacres:** Thank you for the many talks and words of encouragement to not settle for less than God's best for my life.

In memory of my grandfather, **Oswald S. Welsh, Sr.**: As a pre-teen, my siblings and I had to go door-to-door handing out flyers for your real-estate business. It taught me that when you want to win, you have to work hard and do whatever it takes. Thank you for our chocolate chip mint ice cream with rainbow sprinkles conversations and for being one of the first persons to support me when I got started in business. I miss you so much.

In memory of my grandmothers, **Hyacinth Welsh** and **Mavis Campbell:** Thank you for being a blessing in my life. You both supported, encouraged and let me know that nothing was too good for your granddaughter. My heart wishes you were here.

To my siblings, **Tamyka, Sophia, Rhasaun, Taneike, Tesfa, Amayae, and Tasha:** I am so grateful that we were raised to be close. I love our daily group chats and knowing that our bond is unbreakable. I am ecstatic that we have been able to instill this same love for family into our children.

To my son, **Donte':** My heart sings knowing that God blessed me with you. From the time you were in my womb, you were marked for Greatness. It is because of you that I've pushed forward to do my best, knowing that you were watching me. I speak immeasurable abundance over every area of your life and that you will always find the strength to overcome any obstacles and be the best you that you were created to be. You have your own star; shine brightly.

CONTACT

Tishawa Howard

tishawa@tishawahoward.com

www.tishawahoward.com

- www.facebook.com/TishawaHoward
- www.linkedin.com/in/tishawa-howard-2034296a
- www.instagram.com/tishawa